Ana, Boris, and Balloons 1

Comparison Problems

EzraMath.com

EzraMath: Elementary Education

Word Problems' Comprehension

Colored version: ISBN 978-1-7352931-0-3

Black and white version: ISBN 978-1-7352931-5-8

Table of Contents

Vocabulary

Parameter (or label)	*A letter, two letters, or a word that represents a number*
A unit of measure	*It tells us what we are counting*
Equation	*Math sentence with an equal sign*
$>$	Greater than
$<$	Less than
$\geq$	Greater than or equal to
$\leq$	Less than or equal to
Inequality	*Math sentence having $>, <, \geq,$ or $\leq$ sign*
*The number **exceeds 5 by 3***	*It is 3 more than 5*
Two times as many as 5	5×2 or $5 + 5$
Twice as many as 5	5×2 or $5 + 5$
Difference	*In math, the difference between 3 and 5 is 2 since $5 - 3 = 2$*

The Structure of the Book

The book has 50 one-step comparison problems that talk about Ana, Boris, and their balloons.

The approach concentrates readers' attention on math vocabulary.

The problems use various mathematical operations:
addition (+) *and* subtraction (-),

greater than (>) *and* less than (<),

equals (=),

equals or greater than (≥) *and* equals or less than (≤),

the simplest multiplication *(x) and* division *(÷).*

You may solve problems on a basic or advanced level.

On a basic level, *you will make an illustration, find an answer, and display a number sentence.*

On an advanced level, *you will create and analyze* **equations** *and* **inequalities** *and, from the list, choose* **the strategy** *that helped you solve a problem.*

To get the most from this book, *complete all the activities, basic and advanced.*

The next few pages will explain each activity in detail.

Basic Problem-Solving

*Read and **illustrate** all problems.*

- *When pictures show some balloons but need more or fewer (less) to match the problem, add missing drawings of balloons and cross out extra balloons if needed.*
- *When a problem has several solutions, draw an illustration for one of the answers.*

***If a problem is challenging, use counters** to model it.*
*Use two erasers to represent **Ana** and **Boris**. Label them with the letters **A** and **B**.*

Place counters in a line *next to **A**.*   A ◯ ◯ ◯ ◯

Place counters in a line *next to **B**.*   B ◯ ◯ ◯

Adjust the number of counters to fit your problem.

***After solving problems**, **fill in the blanks** in the answer sentences. When several answers are proposed, **cross out** all incorrect answers and **circle** correct ones.*

*Finally, **write your solution—a number sentence** in a circle on the right-hand side of the page.*

The following page will explain how to fill in the circles correctly.

Basic Level: Challenges in Circles

In Circles

Write number sentences that lead to correct answers.

If 4 is the answer to a problem, 4 must be written after sign 'equals':

$$\underline{\hspace{3cm}} = 4$$

A number sentence in a circle must demonstrate how the answer 4 was obtained using the numbers from the problem.

Examples: $(3+1=4)$ $(7-3=4)$ $(8÷2=4)$ $(2×2=4)$

Incorrect examples are shown below.

$$3+4=7 \qquad 4-1=3 \qquad 4×2=8$$

Avoid such sentences because they do not show how to calculate the answer 4.

In these sentences, 4 appears in the calculation instead of being the final result, = 4.

Advanced Problem-Solving: Models

Illustrations to problems can be quite different. An illustration on the title page shows Ana and Boris with their balloons but does not help us solve problems.

The illustrations for problems are not like that. Instead of drawing children, you will draw the balloons mentioned in the problems.

To better visualize comparison, you will draw balloons under one another.

Your illustrations will show what numbers are involved in the problems and help you better understand each comparison case. Such illustrations are called **visual models** and model the values in the problems.

Problem solving involves various types of models.

Models can help you solve the most challenging problems and explain your thinking to others.

When you play out a problem using counters, you are using **a model with counters**.

Equations and inequalities that present a problem in the shortest way are also called models.

Now, let's make some equations and inequalities!

Making Equations and Inequalities

*In this book, we can shorten each problem by using labels **A** and **B** when talking about kids' balloons.*

*   **A** *means the number of balloons related to Ana,*
    B *means the number of balloons related to Boris.*

*Labels **A** and **B** also have another name: **parameters**.*

*With parameter **A**, you can shorten the sentence, **Ana has 5 balloons**, to **A = 5 balloons**.*

Furthermore! You can shorten a measuring unit, balloon to just one letter followed by a dot:

$$A = 5 \text{ b.}$$

Now, you understand how to shorten any problems!

Boris has 2 balloons fewer (less) than Ana.	$B = A - 2 \text{ b.}$
How many balloons does Boris have?	$B = ? \text{ b.}$
Ana has more than 5 balloons.	$A > 5 \text{ b.}$
Boris has 8 balloons or less.	$B \leq 8 \text{ b.}$
Ana has at least 4 balloons.	$A \geq 4 \text{ b.}$
Boris poked less balloons than Ana.	$B < A$
Ana lost 3 more balloons than Boris.	$A = B + 3 \text{ b.}$

Challenges in Banners

Banners on the bottom of each page have true and false math sentences.

> **Circle** *correct math sentences.*

$$\boxed{2+1=3}$$ (circled)

> **Cross out** *incorrect math sentences.*

2+1=1 (crossed out)

It would be so easy if the banners had only numbers!

*The banners in this book have equations and inequalities with parameters **A** and **B**. The values of A and B vary.*

To find whether a math sentence is correct or not, substitute parameters with the numbers they represent:

$A + B = 5$ (circled)

For example,

If $A = 3$ b. and $B = 2$b., then

$A - B = 2$ (crossed out)

   $A + B = 5$ is a correct equation.

   $A - B = 2$ is incorrect since $3 - 2 = 1$.

$A > B$ (circled)

   $A > B$ is correct since $3 > 2$.

   $A < B$ is incorrect since $3 < 2$ is not true.

$A < B$ (crossed out)

The Lines and Grey Boxes

Each problem has lines on the top of the page like the lines below. These lines are for writing a problem in a short way using equations and inequalities.

_____

_____

_____

_____

_____

Equations
Illustration
Counters

On the right-hand side, there is a grey box. After you solve a problem, mark the strategy that helped you the most.

If a problem is very easy and you solve it without aids, cross all three strategies in the box.

If an illustration or counters helped you, circle the word illustration *or the word* counters.

Finally, if the equations and inequalities helped you, circle equations. *Analysis of strategies will help you become a better problem solver.*

Now, you are ready. Start solving the problems!

Problem 1

A = ____ b.

B = A

B = ? b.

'Balloon' is the **measuring unit** for value 7.
The **dot** after **b.** shows that the word **balloon** is abbreviated (shortened) to a single letter, b.

Ana has 7 balloons. Boris has <u>the same number</u> of balloons as Ana. How many balloons does he have?

illustration to the problem

A ○ ○ ○ ○ ○

B ○ ○ ○

Answer: Boris has ____ balloons.

$$A > B \qquad A < B \qquad A = B \qquad B = A$$

Problem 2

___ = ___ ___

B > ____

B = ? b.

First, write what is given in the problem, line by line.

Then, write the question that the problem is asking.

Ana has 6 balloons. Boris has <u>more</u> balloons than Ana. How many balloons might Boris have?

illustration to the problem

A ○ ○ ○ ○

B

$B > 6$

Answer: Boris might have 3, 4, 5, 6, 7, 8, 9, or ____ balloons.

$A > B$ 　　　 $A < B$ 　　　 $A = B$ 　　　 $B > A$

Problem 3

___ = ___ ___

B < ___

*In everyday speech, we often say **less balloons**. In math, we use the word **fewer** for countable things like balloons. This book uses both words to let you get used to the correct math term. **Fewer** means **less**.*

Ana has 5 balloons. Boris has <u>fewer</u> balloons than Ana. How many balloons might Boris have?

illustration to the problem

A ○ ○ ○ ○

B

$B < 5$

Answer: Boris might have 3, 4, 5, 6, 7, ____, ____, or ____ balloons.

$A > B$ $\qquad$ $A < B$ $\qquad$ $A = B$ $\qquad$ $B > A$

Problem 4

A = ___ __

B = A + 2 b.

Equations
Illustration
Counters

Ana has 7 balloons. Boris has <u>2 more</u> balloons than Ana. What is the number of balloons that Boris has?

illustration to the problem

A $\quad \circ \quad \circ \quad \circ \quad \circ$

B

$7 + 2 = 9$

Answer: The number of Boris' balloons is ____ .

$$A > B \qquad A < B \qquad A = 7 \qquad B = A + 2$$

14

Problem 5

_____

_____

_____

_____

_____

Boris had 8 balloons. Ana had <u>as many balloons as</u> Boris. How many balloons did she have?

illustration to the problem

A ○ ○ ○ ○

B

$A = B$

Answer: Ana had _____ balloons.

$B > A$ $\qquad$ $B < A$ $\qquad$ $B = A + 7$ $\qquad$ $A = B - 8$

Problem 6

_____

_____

_____

_____

_____

Equations
Illustration
Counters

Boris has 6 balloons. Boris has <u>more</u> balloons than Ana. How many balloons might Ana have?

A ○ ○ ○ ○

B

Answer: Ana might have 3, 4, 5, 6, 7, 8, _____, _____, or _____ balloons.

$B > A$ $B < A$ $B = A$ $A \leq B$

Problem 7

_____

_____

_____

_____

Ana has 5 balloons. Ana has <u>the same number</u> of balloons as Boris <u>or more</u>. How many balloons might Boris have?

A

B

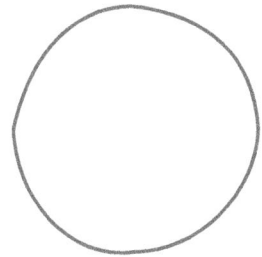

Answer: Boris might have 8, 7, 6, 5, 4, 3, ____, ____, or ____ balloons.

$$A > B \qquad A \leq B \qquad B \leq A \qquad A \geq B$$

Problem 8

_____

_____

_____

_____

_____

Equations
Illustration
Counters

Ana has 5 balloons. Boris has <u>2 less</u> balloons than Ana. How many balloons does Boris have?

A ○ ○ ○ ○

B

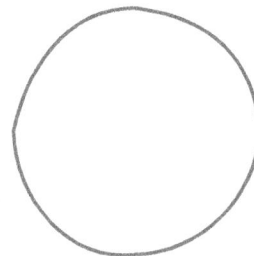

Answer: Boris has _____ balloons.

$$B = 5 + 2 \qquad A = 5 + 2 \qquad A = 5 - 2 \qquad B = 5 - 2$$

Problem 9

_____

_____

_____

_____

_____

Ana has 4 balloons. She has <u>fewer</u> balloons than Boris.
How many balloons might Boris have?

A ○ ○ ○ ○

B

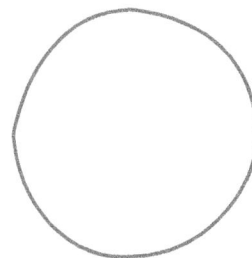

Answer: Boris might have 3, 4, 5, 6, 7, ____, ____, or ____ balloons.

$$B > A \qquad B < A \qquad A = 4 \qquad B < 4$$

Problem 10

_____

_____

_____

_____

_____

Boris has 4 balloons. Ana has <u>2 more</u> balloons than Boris. What is the number of balloons that Ana has?

A ○ ○ ○ ○

B

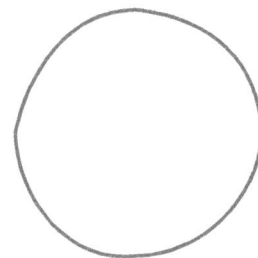

Answer: The number of Ana's balloons is _____ .

$$A > B \qquad A - B = 2 \qquad A = B + 2 \qquad A = 4 + 2$$

Problem 11

_____

_____

_____

_____

Equations
Illustration
Counters

Boris has 5 balloons. He has <u>1 more</u> balloon than Ana. How many balloons does Ana have?

A

B ○ ○ ○ ○

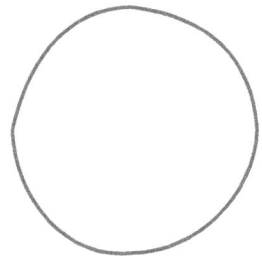

Answer: Ana has _____ balloons.

$$B > A \qquad B < A \qquad B = A + 5 \qquad A = B + 1$$

What is 'exceeds by 3'?

- *Exceeds by 3 is another way to say '3 more'.*

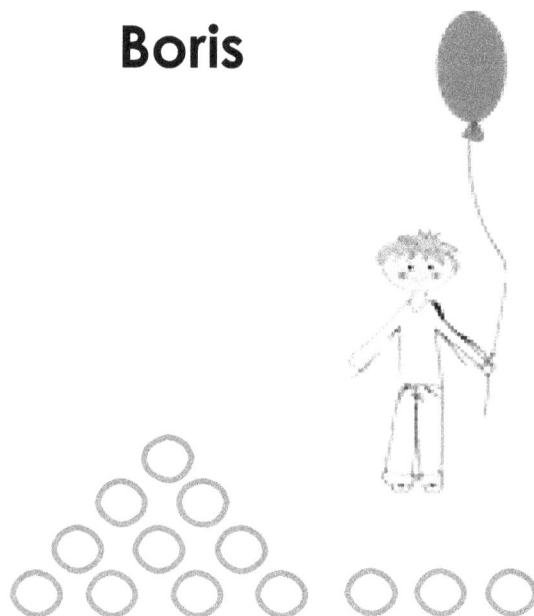

Ana   **Boris**

$$A > B \qquad B < A \qquad B = A + 3 \qquad B = A - 3$$

Problem 12

_____

_____

_____

_____

_____

Equations
Illustration
Counters

Ana has 3 balloons. The number of Boris' balloons <u>exceeds</u> Ana's <u>by 2</u>. How many balloons does he have?

A

B ○ ○ ○ ○

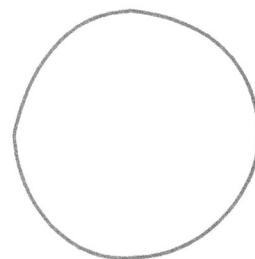

Answer: Boris has _____ balloons.

$$3 - 1 = 1 \qquad B = 3 + 2 \qquad A = B - 2 \qquad B = A + 2$$

Problem 13

_____

_____

_____

A − B = ? b.

_____

_____

Boris has 5 balloons. The number of Ana's balloons <u>exceeds</u> Boris' <u>by 3</u>. How many more balloons does Ana have than Boris?

A ○ ○ ○ ○

B

Answer: Ana has _____ balloons more than Boris.

$$B = 5 \qquad A = 8 \qquad B - A = 3 \qquad A - B = 3$$

Problem 14

_____

_____

_____

_____

_____

Equations
Illustration
Counters

Ana has 6 balloons. The number of her balloons <u>exceeds</u> the number of Boris' balloons <u>by 4</u>. How many balloons does Boris have?

A ○ ○ ○ ○

B

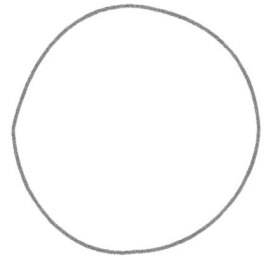

Answer: Boris has ____ balloons.

$A > B$ $B > A$ $B = 4$ $A = 6$

Problem 15

Equations
Illustration
Counters

Ana has 6 balloons. Ana has <u>1 less</u> balloon than Boris. What is the number of balloons that Boris has?

A ○ ○ ○ ○

B

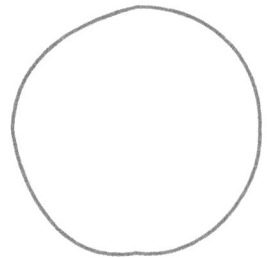

Answer: The number of Boris' balloons is ____ .

$$6 + 1 = 7 \qquad 6 - 1 = 5 \qquad A = B - 1 \qquad B = A - 1$$

Problem 16

_____

Equations Illustration Counters

There were *some* balloons on the table. Ana and Boris took an <u>equal number</u> of balloons. Boris took 4 balloons. What is the number of balloons that Ana took?

A

B

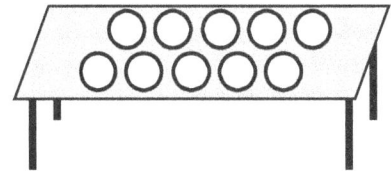

Answer: The number of balloons Ana took is _____.

$$A + B = 10 \qquad A = B \qquad B = 4 \qquad A = B - 4$$

'Twice as Many' Problems

What is **2 times as many**?

- **Two times as many** means a number is taken 2 times.

- **Two times as many as 4 balloons** means 4 balloons and then again 4 balloons.

- **Twice as many** is the same as **two times as many**.

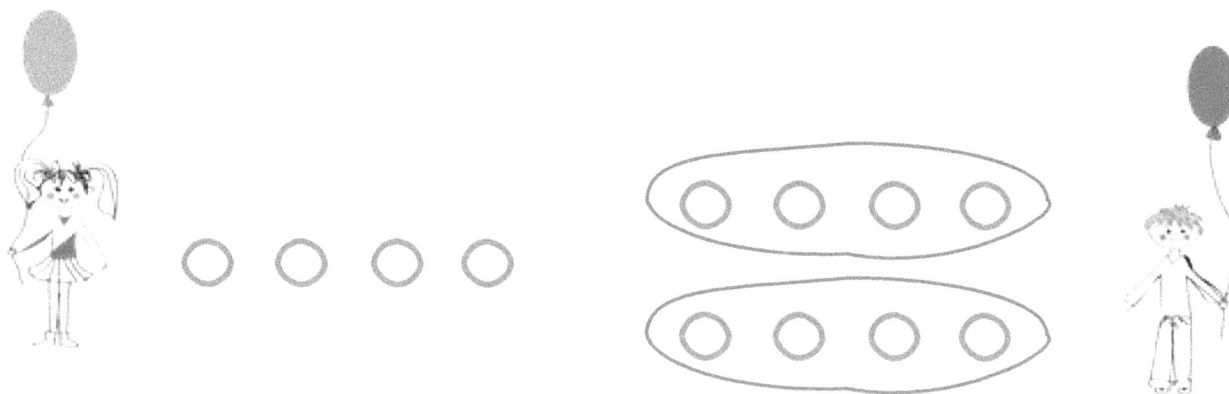

$$A + A = 10 \qquad 2 \times A = B \qquad B \div 2 = 4 \qquad B = A - 2$$

Problem 17

_____

_____

_____

_____

Equations
Illustration
Counters

Ana has 3 balloons. Boris has <u>2 times as many</u> balloons as Ana. How many balloons does Boris have?

A

B

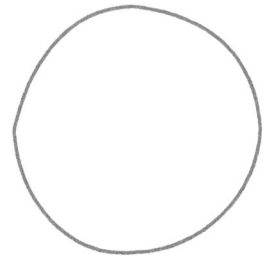

Answer: Boris has ____ balloons.

$$B > A \qquad B = A + A \qquad B = 3 + 2 \qquad B = 3 + 3$$

Problem 18

_____

_____

_____

_____

_____

Equations
Illustration
Counters

Boris had 4 balloons. Ana had <u>twice as many</u> balloons as Boris. How many balloons did Ana have?

A

B ○ ○ ○ ○

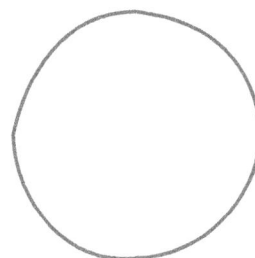

Answer: Ana had _____ balloons.

$$B < A \qquad B = A + A \qquad B = 4 + 4 \qquad A = B + B$$

Problem 19

Equations
Illustration
Counters

Boris has 5 balloons. Ana has <u>3 fewer</u> balloons than Boris. How many balloons does Ana have?

A

B

Answer: Ana has ____ balloons.

$$5 - 3 = 2 \qquad B < A \qquad B = A + 3 \qquad A = B - 3$$

Problem 20

_____

_____

_____

_____

Equations
Illustration
Counters

Ana has 7 balloons. Boris has <u>the same number</u> of balloons as Ana or <u>1</u> <u>fewer</u>. What is the number of balloons that Boris might have?

A ○ ○ ○ ○

B

Answer: Boris might have 1, 2, 3, 4, 5, 6, or 7 balloons.

$$B = A - 1 \qquad B \geq A \qquad B = A \qquad B \leq A$$

Problem 21

A + B ≤ 10 b.
A = __ __
B =
B = ? b.

Together, kids cannot take more than 10 balloons from the table. A + B shows how many balloons the kids took in all. That number cannot be more than 10.

There were 10 balloons on the table. Ana took 3 of them. Boris took <u>as many balloons as</u> Ana. How many did Boris take?

A

B

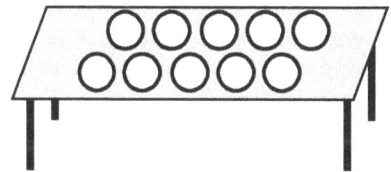

Answer: Boris took ____ balloons.

$$A > B \qquad B < 10 \qquad A = B + 3 \qquad B = 10 - 3$$

Problem 22

There were 10 balloons on the table. Boris took 3 of them. Ana took <u>twice as many</u> balloons as Boris. How many did Ana take?

A

B

Answer: Ana took ____ balloons.

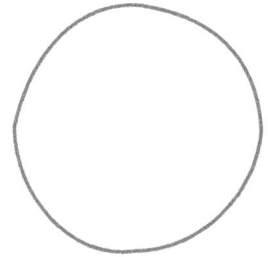

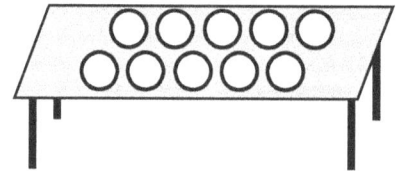

$$A + B \leq 10 \qquad A = 3 + 3 \qquad B = 3 + 3 \qquad B = 3$$

Problem 23

_____

_____

_____

_____

Equations
Illustration
Counters

Ana has 8 balloons. Boris has <u>2</u> balloons <u>fewer</u> than Ana. How many balloons does Boris have?

A

B

Answer: Boris has _____ balloons.

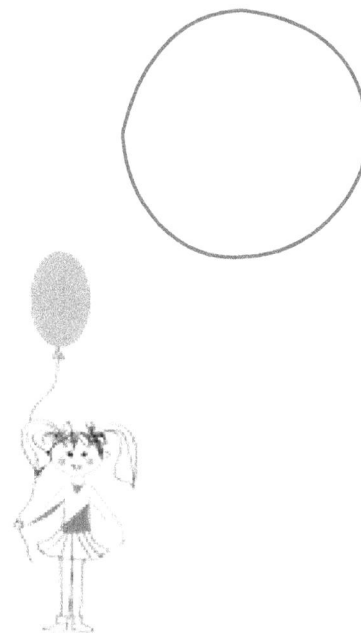

$$A > B \qquad A = 8 \qquad B = A + 2 \qquad B = A - 2$$

Problem 24

A = ___ __

B = ___ __

A − B = ? b.

To find the difference between A and B, subtract (take away) a smaller number (B = 3 b.) from a greater number (A = 4 b.). In this problem, the difference between A and B is **A − B**.

Ana has 4 balloons. Boris has 3 balloons. What is the difference between the numbers of balloons Ana and Boris have?

A ○ ○ ○ ○

B

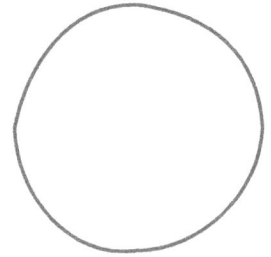

Answer: The difference between the numbers of balloons is ____.

$$B = A - 1 \qquad A = B + 1 \qquad A - B = 1 \qquad B - A = 1$$

Problem 25

_____

_____

_____

_____

_____

Ana has 5 balloons. Boris has <u>2 more</u> balloons than Ana. What is the number of the boy's balloons?

A

B

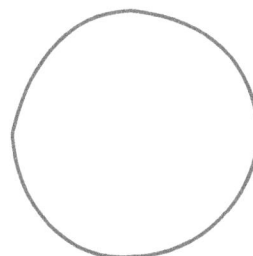

Answer: The number of Boris' balloons is ____.

$$A = B + 5 \qquad B = A + 5 \qquad A = B + 2 \qquad B = A + 2$$

Problem 26

_____

_____

_____

_____

_____

Equations
Illustration
Counters

Boris has 7 balloons. Boris has at least <u>2 more</u> balloons than Ana. What is the number of Ana's balloons?

A ○ ○ ○ ○

B

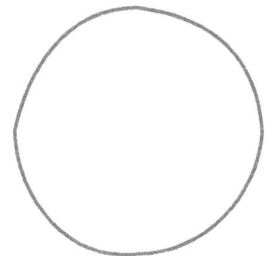

Answer: Ana might have _____, or

_____ balloons.

$$B = A + 2 \qquad A < 7 \qquad A < 6 \qquad B - A \geq 2$$

38

Problem 27

A = ___ __

A = 2 × B   or   B = A ÷ 2

B = ? b.

When A = 2 × B, then B makes a half of A. If we divide A into two equal parts, we will get B. In mathematics, we write,
$$B = A \div 2.$$

Ana had 2 balloons. She had <u>twice as many</u> balloons as Boris. What is the number of Boris' balloons?

A

B

Answer: The number of Boris' balloons is ____.

$$B < A \qquad A = 2 \qquad A = B + B \qquad B = A + A$$

Problem 28

_____

_____

_____

_____

_____

Ana has 1 balloon. The <u>difference</u> between the number of balloons that the kids have <u>is 3</u>. How many balloons does Boris have?

A

B

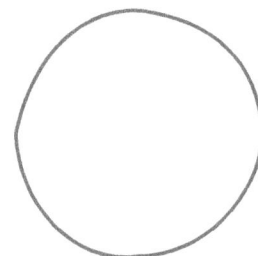

Answer: Boris has _____ balloons.

$$B - A = 1 \qquad B - A = 3 \qquad B = A - 3 \qquad B = A + 3$$

Problem 29

_____

_____

_____

_____

_____

Equations
Illustration
Counters

Boris has 9 balloons. Ana has <u>2</u> balloons <u>fewer</u> than Boris. What is the number of her balloons?

A

B

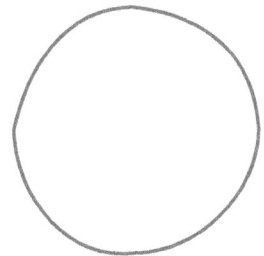

Answer: The number of Ana's balloons is ____.

$$A = 9 - 2 \qquad A = 9 + 2 \qquad B = A - 2 \qquad A = B - 2$$

Problem 30

_____

_____

_____

_____

_____

Ana has 5 balloons. Boris has <u>2 times as many</u> balloons as Ana. How many balloons does he have?

A ○ ○ ○ ○

B

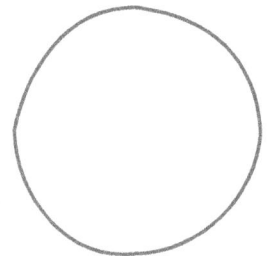

Answer: Boris has _____ balloons.

$$B < A \qquad 5 + 5 = 10 \qquad B = A + 2 \qquad B = A + A$$

Problem 31

Ana has 10 balloons. She has 2 times as many balloons as Boris. How many balloons does he have?

A

B

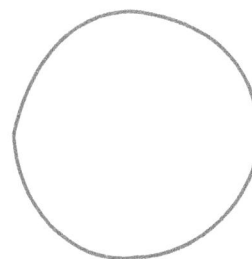

Answer: Boris has _____ balloons.

$$10 - 2 = 8 \quad 5 + 5 = 10 \quad A = B + B \quad B = A + A$$

Problem 32

_____

_____

_____

_____

_____

Equations
Illustration
Counters

There were 8 balloons on the table. Boris took some of them. Ana took 3. She took fewer ballons than Boris. How many balloons did Boris take?

A

B   ○   ○   ○

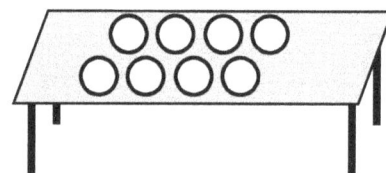

Answer: Boris took _____ or _____ balloons.

$$B - A = 3 \qquad A + B < 10 \qquad B = 5 \qquad B = 6$$

Problem 33

_____

_____

_____

_____

_____

Equations
Illustration
Counters

Boris has 10 balloons. Ana has 2 fewer balloons than Boris. How many balloons does Ana have?

A

B

Answer: Ana has _____ balloons.

$$B - A = 2 \qquad A - B = 2 \qquad B = A + 2 \qquad A = B + 2$$

Problem 34

_____

Ana bought 1 balloon. Boris bought twice as many balloons as Ana. What is the number of balloons he bought?

A

B

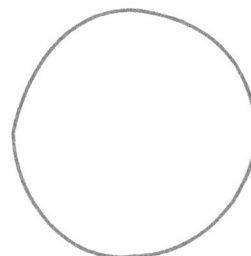

Answer: The number of balloons Boris bought is _____.

$$B < A \qquad A > B \qquad A = B + B \qquad B = A + A$$

Problem 35

A > 0 b. and B _____

A = 2 b.

Since each child has some balloons, we need to create one inequality for each child.
We start with writing about A,
A > 0 b. and then writing about B.

Each child has some balloons. Ana has 2 balloons. The number of Boris' balloons is less than Ana's. How many does Boris have?

A

B

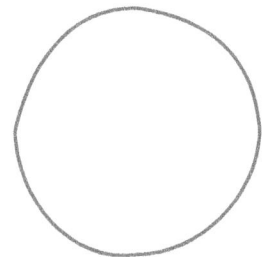

Answer: Boris has _____ balloons.

$A > B$ $A < B$ $A \geq 1$ $B \geq 1$

Problem 36

_____

_____

_____

_____

_____

Ana has 7 balloons. Boris has 6 balloons. How many fewer balloons does Boris have than Ana?

A ○ ○ ○ ○

B

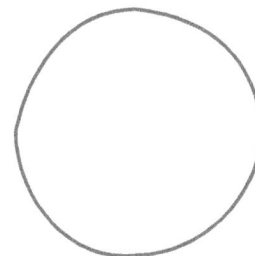

Answer: Boris has ____ balloon fewer than Ana.

$$A - B = 7 \qquad A < B \qquad B - A = 7 \qquad B > A$$

Problem 37

_____

_____

_____

_____

_____

Equations
Illustration
Counters

Ana has 7 balloons. Boris has 2 balloons fewer than Ana. How many more balloons does Ana have than Boris?

A

B

Answer: Ana has _____ more balloons than Boris.

$$A - B = 2 \qquad B - A = 2 \qquad A > B \qquad B < A$$

Problem 38

_____

_____

_____

_____

_____

There were 6 balloons on the table. Boris took 3 balloons. Ana took 4 balloons. What is the difference between the number of balloons Ana and Boris took?

A ○ ○ ○ ○

B

Answer: The difference is ____. However, the problem _____ because _____ .

$$A + B = 7 \qquad A = B - 1 \qquad A - B = 1 \qquad A + B < 7$$

Problem 39

_____

_____

_____

_____

_____

There were 10 balloons on the table. Ana took 3 of them. Then Boris took a few balloons too. He took more balloons than Ana. How many did he take?

A

B

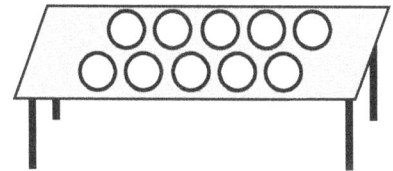

Answer: Boris took ____, ____, ____, or ____ balloons.

$$A = 3 \qquad A < B \qquad A + B \leq 10 \qquad B > 3$$

Problem 40

_____

_____

_____

_____

Equations
Illustration
Counters

Ana has 1 balloon. Boris has 5 more balloons than Ana. What is the number of Boris' balloons?

A

B

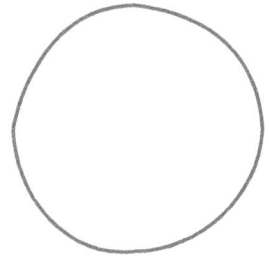

Answer: The number of Boris' balloons is _____.

$$B = A + 5 \quad A = B - 5 \quad A - B = 1 \quad B - A = 1$$

Problem 41

_____

_____

_____

_____

Equations
Illustration
Counters

Ana has 7 balloons. Boris has 5 balloons. How many more balloons does Ana have than Boris?

A

B

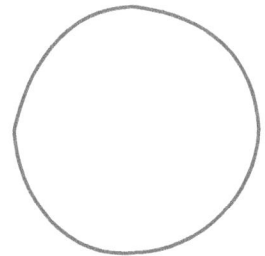

Answer: Ana has _____ balloons more than Boris.

$$B > A \qquad B < A \qquad A = B + 2 \qquad B = A + 2$$

Problem 42

_____

_____

_____

_____

_____

Boris has 7 balloons. Ana has 3 balloons fewer than Boris. How many more balloons does Boris have than Ana?

A

B ○ ○ ○ ○

Answer: Boris has ____ more balloons than Ana.

$$B = A + 3 \qquad B = A - 3 \qquad A = B + 7 \qquad A = B - 7$$

Problem 43

_____

_____

_____

_____

_____

Equations
Illustration
Counters

Ana has 9 balloons. Boris has 3 balloons. How many fewer balloons does Boris have than Ana?

A

B

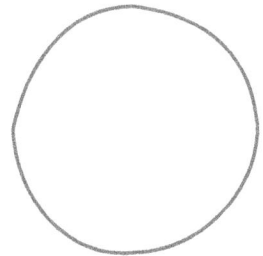

Answer: Boris has _____ fewer balloons than Ana.

$$A > B \qquad A < B \qquad A = B + 6 \qquad B = A - 6$$

Problem 44

_____

_____

_____

_____

Equations
Illustration
Counters

Boris inflated 8 balloons. He inflated 2 more balloons than Ana. How many balloons did Ana inflate?

A

B ○ ○ ○ ○

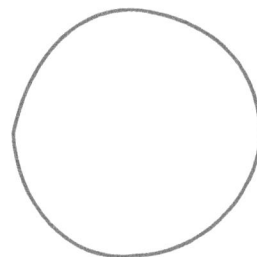

Answer: Ana inflated ____ balloons.

$$B > A \qquad B < A \qquad B = A + 2 \qquad A = B + 2$$

Problem 45

_____

_____

_____

_____

Equations
Illustration
Counters

Boris painted 9 balloons. Ana painted an equal number of balloons. How many balloons did she paint?

A

B

Answer: Ana painted _____ balloons.

$$B > A \qquad B < A \qquad B \leq A \qquad A \leq B$$

57

Problem 46

_____

_____

_____

_____

Ana has 8 balloons. Boris has 6 balloons. By how much does the number of Ana's balloons exceed 5?

A ○ ○ ○ ○

B

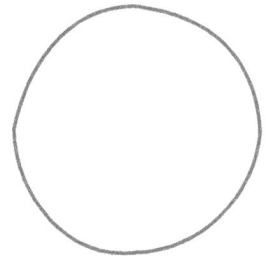

Answer: The number of Ana's balloons exceeds 5 by

____.

$A > 5$ $5 < A$ $6 > B$ $B < 8$

Problem 47

Boris and Ana have some balloons. Ana has 3 balloons. The difference between the numbers of the children's balloons is 2. How many balloons does Boris have?

A

B

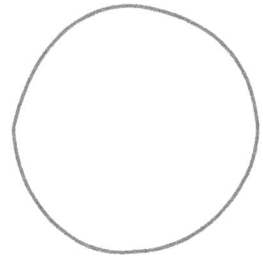

Answer: Boris has ____ or ____ balloons.

$$B = A - 2 \qquad B = A + 2 \qquad A = B + 2 \qquad A = B - 2$$

Problem 48

_____

_____

_____

_____

Equations
Illustration
Counters

Boris hid 4 balloons. Ana hid 2 times as many balloons. How many balloons did Ana hide?

A

B ○ ○ ○ ○

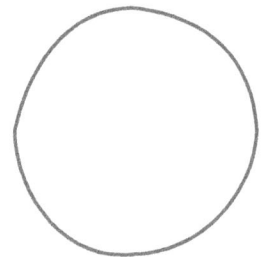

Answer: Ana hid ____ balloons.

$$B + B = A \quad B = A + A \quad B = A + 2 \quad A = B + 2$$

Problem 49

_____

_____

_____

_____

_____

Equations
Illustration
Counters

Ana has 7 balloons. Boris has 5 balloons fewer than Ana. How many balloons does Boris have? What is the difference between the numbers of kids' balloons?

A

B

Answer: Boris has _____ balloons. The difference between the number of balloons is _____.

$$A \leq B \qquad B \leq A \qquad A = B + 5 \qquad A = B - 5$$

Problem 50

_____

_____

_____

_____

_____

Equations
Illustration
Counters

Boris had as many balloons as Ana. Together they had fewer than 9 balloons. How many more balloons did Boris have than Ana?

A ○ ○ ○ ○

B

Answer: Boris had ____ balloons more than Ana.

$$A + B < 9 \qquad A - B = 0 \qquad B - A = 0 \qquad 9 > A$$

Farewell

You completed the first book from *Ana, Boris, and Balloons* sequel.

The following books will introduce 'Combine' and 'Change' problems. The sequel covers word problems' vocabulary in depth and prepares students for solving challenging story problems including logic problems.

Let problem-solving power be with you. Good luck!

Answers

	Answers and *True* Banners	Circle	Shortened Problems
#1	**7** (3) $A = B$ (4) $B = A$		A = 7 b. B = A B = ? b.
#2	~~3, 4, 5, 6~~, 7, 8, 9, **10**. *Greater numbers can be as well.* (2) $A < B$ (4) $B > A$		A = 6 b. B > A B = ? b.
#3	3, 4, ~~5, 6, 7~~, **2**, **1**, or **0** (1) $A > B$	$B < 5$	A = 5 b. B < A B = ? b.
#4	**9** (2) $A < B$ (3) $A = 7$ (4) $B = A + 2$		A = 7 b. B = A + 2 b. B = ? b.
#5	**8** All banners are incorrect.	8 = 8	B = 8 b. A = B A = ? b.
#6	3, 4, 5, ~~6, 7, 8~~, **2**, **1**, or **0** (1) $B > A$	$A < 6$	B = 6 b. A < B (B > A) A = ? b.
#7	~~8, 7, 6~~, 5, 4, 3, **2**, **1**, or **0** (3) $B \leq A$ (4) $A \geq B$	$B \leq 5$	A = 5 b. B ≤ A (B = A or B < A) B = ? b.

Answers and *True* Banners	Circle	Shortened Problems
#8 **3** (4) $B = 5 - 2$		A = 5 b. B = A − 2 b. B = ? b.
#9 ~~3, 4~~, 5, 6, 7, **8**, **9**, or **10** *Greater numbers can be.* (1) $B > A$ (3) $A = 4$	$B > 4$	A = 4 b. B > A (A < B) B = ? b.
#10 **6** All banners are correct.	$4 + 2 = 6$	B = 4 b. A = B + 2 b. A = ? b.
#11 **4** (1) $B > A$	$5 - 1 = 4$	B = 5 b. A = B − 1 b. A = ? b.
Exceeds by 3 (3) $B = A + 3$		
#12 **5** (2) $B = 3 + 2$ (3) $B = A + 2$ (4) $A = B - 2$	$3 + 2 = 5$	A = 3 b. B = A + 2 b. B = ? b.
#13 **3** (1) $B = 5$ (2) $A = 8$ (4) $A - B = 3$		B = 5 b. A = B + 3 b. A − B = ? b.
#14 **2** (1) $A > B$ (4) $A = 6$	$6 - 4 = 2$	A = 6 b. B = A − 4 b. B = ? b.

Answers and *True* Banners	Circle	Shortened Problems
#15 **7** (1) $6 + 1 = 7$ (3) $A = B - 1$	$6 + 1 = 7$	A = 6 b. B = A + 1 b. B = ? b.
#16 **4** (2) $A = B$ (3) $B = 4$		B = 4 b. A = B A = ? b.

Twice as Many
     (2) $2 \times A = B$ (3) $B \div 2 = 4$

Answers and *True* Banners	Circle	Shortened Problems
#17 **6** (1) $B > A$ (2) $B = A + A$ (4) $B = 3 + 3$	$2 \times 3 = 6$	A = 3 b. B = 2 × A B = ? b.
#18 **8** (1) $B < A$ (4) $A = B + B$	$4 \times 2 = 8$	B = 4 b. A = 2 × B A = ? b.
#19 **2** (1) $5 - 3 = 2$ (3) $B = A + 3$ (4) $A = B - 3$		B = 5 b. A = B – 3 b. A = ? b.
#20 ~~1,2,3,4,5,~~ 6,7 (1) $B = A - 1$ (3) $B = A$		A = 7 b. B = A or B = A – 1 b. B = ? b.
#21 **3** (2) $B < 10$		A + B ≤ 10 b. A = 3 b. B = A B = ? b.

Answers and *True* Banners	Circle	Shortened Problems
#22 **6** (1) $A + B \leq 10$ (2) $A = 3 + 3$ (4) $B = 3$	$3 \times 2 = 6$	A + B ≤ 10 b. B = 3 b. A = 2 × B A = ? b.
#23 **6** (1) $A > B$ (2) $A = 8$ (4) $B = A - 2$	$8 - 2 = 6$	A = 8 b. B = A − 2 b. B = ? b.
#24 **1** (1) $B = A - 1$ (2) $A = B + 1$ (3) $A - B = 1$	$4 - 3 = 1$	A = 4 b. B = 3 b. A − B = ? b.
#25 **7** (4) $B = A + 2$	$5 + 2 = 7$	A = 5 b. B = A + 2 b. B = ? b.
#26 **0,1,2,3,4,5** (2) $A < 7$ (3) $A < 6$ (4) $B - A \geq 2$	$A \leq 5$ or $A < 6$	B = 7 b. A ≤ B − 2 A = ? b.
#27 **1** (1) $B < A$ (2) $A = 2$ (3) $A = B + B$	$2 \div 2 = 1$	A = 2 b. A = 2 × B or B = A ÷ 2 B = ? b.
#28 **4** (2) $B - A = 3$ (4) $B = A + 3$	$1 + 3 = 4$	A = 1 b. B = A − 3 b. or B = A + 3b. B = ? b.

Answers and *True* Banners	Circle	Shortened Problems
#29 **7** (1) $A = 9 - 2$ (4) $A = B - 2$	$9 - 2 = 7$	B = 9 b. A = B − 2 b. A = ? b.
#30 **10** (2) $5 + 5 = 10$ (4) $B = A + A$	$5 \times 2 = 10$	A = 5 b. B = 2 × A B = ? b.
#31 **5** (2) $5 + 5 = 10$ (3) $A = B + B$	$10 \div 2 = 5$	A = 10 b. A = 2 × B or B = A ÷ 2 B = ? b.
#32 **4 or 5** (2) $A + B < 10$ (3) $B = 5$		A + B ≤ 8 b. A = 3 b. B > A B = ? b.
#33 **8** (1) $B - A = 2$ (3) $B = A + 2$	$10 - 2 = 8$	B = 10 b. A = B − 2 b. A = ? b.
#34 **2** (3) $A = B + B$	$1 \times 2 = 2$	A = 1 b. B = 2 × A B = ? b.
#35 **1** (1) $A > B$ (3) $A \geq 1$ (4) $B \geq 1$	$B < 2,$ $B > 0$	A > 0 b. and B > 0 b. A = 2 b. B < A B = ? b.
#36 **1** All answers are incorrect.	$7 - 6 = 1$	A = 7 b. B = 6 b. A − B = ? b.

Answers and *True* Banners	Circle	Shortened Problems
#37 **2** (1) $A - B = 2$ (3) $A > B$ (4) $B < A$		A = 7 b. B = A – 2 b. A – B = ? b.
#38 Although the difference is 1 balloon, the problem has no solution. There are 6 balloons in all. So, the children could not take 4 and 3 balloons. (1) $A + B = 7$ (3) $A - B = 1$ (4) A + B < 7		A + B ≤ 6 b. A = 4 b. B = 3 b. A – B = ? b.
#39 **4, 5, 6,** or **7** All answers are correct.		A + B < 10 b. A = 3 b. B > A B = ? b.
#40 **6** (1) $B = A + 5$ (2) $A = B - 5$	$1 + 5 = 6$	A = 1 b. B = A + 5 b. B = ? b.
#41 **2** (2) $B < A$ (3) $A = B + 2$	$7 - 5 = 2$	A = 7 b. B = 5 b. A – B = ? b.
#42 **3** (1) $B = A + 3$		B = 7 b. A = B – 3 b. B – A = ? b.

Answers and *True* Banners		Circle	Shortened Problems
#43	**6** (1) $A > B$ (3) $A = B + 6$ (4) $B = A - 6$	$9 - 3 = 6$	A = 9 b. B = 3 b. A – B = ? b.
#44	**6** (1) $B > A$ (3) $B = A + 2$	$8 - 2 = 6$	B = 8 b. A = B – 2 b. A = ? b.
#45	**9** (3) $B \leq A$ (4) $A \leq B$		B = 9 b. A = B A = ? b.
#46	**3** (1) $A > 5$ (2) $5 < A$ (4) $B < 8$	$8 - 5 = 3$	A = 8 b. B = 6 b. A – 5b. = ? b.
#47	**1** or **5** All answers are correct.	$3 - 2 = 1$ $3 + 2 = 5$	A > 0 b. and B > 0 b. A = 3 b. B = A + 3 b. or B = A – 3 b. B = ? b.
#48	**8** (1) $B + B = A$	$4 \times 2 = 8$	B = 4 b. A = 2 × B A = ? b.
#49	**2** and **5** (2) $B \leq A$ (3) $A = B + 5$		A = 7 b. B = A – 5 b. B = ? b. A – B = ? b.
#50	**0** All answers are correct.		B = A A + B < 9 b. B – A = ? b.

www.ingramcontent.com/pod-product-compliance
Lightning Source LLC
Chambersburg PA
CBHW080940030426
42339CB00008B/465